SALES FUNDAMENTALS
FOR
TECHNICAL SPECIALISTS

JANNE V. KORHONEN

Preface

This book is dedicated to Finnish engineers, who have lifted the competitiveness of the Finnish economy to the international top.

I would like to thank Anne Soininen for the English translation of this book.

Special thanks go out to the people I interviewed: John Care, Sani Leino, John Bates, Timo Sorri, and Taina Närhi.

I also express my humblest thanks to everyone who pre-ordered this book for their feedback and for the social pressure without which this book may never have become reality.

I am happy to connect with anyone interested in doing business in Finland, Nordics or anywhere around the globe:
www.linkedin.com/in/jannekooo
www.twitter.com/jannekooo

Contents

Preface i

Introduction 1

  Selling remains 1

  Filling the need 2

  The structure of the book 4

  How to learn by reading? 4

Technical specialist as a salesperson 7

  Salespeople are irritating 7

  An extrovert is not a good salesperson 7

  Selling is not working anymore 9

  First, convince yourself 13

Interview: John Care 17

  Are engineers needed in sales? 17

  How does an engineer learn to sell? 18

  Your tips for engineers? 19

Opening the discussion 21

  The bottleneck of sales 21

  Inbound marketing 22

  Social selling 25

  The fallacy of telemarketing 28

Ethos - credibility 31

  Nobody cares about what you say 31

  Elements of trust 32

  Trust is not enough 34

  Serve in advance and for free 39

Interview: Sani Leino..**41**

How has selling changed?....................................41

Why is expertise the key?....................................43

Is cold calling dead?..44

Your tips for engineers?......................................44

Pathos - emotion..**47**

Maybe decisions are not made with the heart?........47

How to create emotions?.....................................49

Story, a backdoor to the mind..............................51

When NO comes out of nowhere...........................55

Interview: John Bates..**57**

What is the role of emotions?...............................57

How to tell a good story?.....................................58

Your tips for engineers?......................................59

Logos - argumentation.....................................**61**

You are selling the wrong thing............................61

Engineer logic is not working...............................63

Getting to the core...65

From technology to the need................................68

Beg for objections..71

Ultimately, the most important thing is...................73

Interview: Timo Sorri..**75**

What is a good sales presentation like?..................75

The weakness of engineers?................................76

What is the best way to develop?..........................77

Your tips for engineers?......................................77

Negotiation skills..**79**

    Let the match begin.. 79

    Life is a negotiation 80

    Power behind everything 82

    Room for negotiation... 84

    Indirect methods 87

    Negotiation style 92

    Negotiation process 95

    Deepening the cooperation...................................100

Interview: Taina Närhi **103**

    Why is negotiating so important?..........................103

    The weakness of engineers?..................................104

    Your tips for engineers? 105

In conclusion.. **107**

    Why should we sell?...107

    This cannot go on 107

    All is better than before...108

    Development keeps on developing 109

    Selling is our obligation 111

References and recommended reading................. **113**

Introduction

Selling remains

What in your opinion is the most significant career skill that you could learn, in order to secure your future in working life? A skill that would not become obsolete in a few years' time, but would, for the rest of your life, yield interest on the time you invested in gaining it?

In January 2016, the World Economic Forum published an extensive survey mapping new job categories and functions that would become critically important by the year 2020. The survey included interviews with 371 strategy and HR executives of large companies, representing more than 13 million employees. The same two job types stood out across all industries and geographies. The first was that of a data analyst and the second that of a specialized sales representative.

"The second are specialized sales representatives, as practically every industry will need to become skilled in commercialising and explaining their offerings to business or government clients and consumers, either due to the innovative technical nature of the products themselves or due to new client targets with which the company is not yet familiar, or both," the survey explained.

Automation and outsourcing will soon greatly reduce the number of white-collar jobs from the Western world. In IT, for example, data centers are being rapidly automated and large-scale projects and a significant share of product developments can be outsourced to countries where costs are lower. What remains is the agile development conducted close to the customer business.

> *"Before, the focus of all work was on building products, in the future, the focus is on building customer relationships."*
> *- Esko Kilpi*

After robotization, people are left with creative problem solving, i.e. tasks that need recognizing situations (problems and opportunities) where value can be created together with the customer. This could also be called selling. Sales skills will therefore be at the core of all work in the future. This applies to a waiter, as well as to an engineer.

Filling the need

Two years ago in November 2014, I established the Meetup group Sales Engineering Finland (www.salesengfi.org). I called out in social media for other Finnish engineers interested in selling. There are now over 450 of us, more than in any other group around the same subject on a global scale.

We did not establish an association, but gathered around a shared field of interest through social media. Sales Engineering Finland is a good example of how digitalization allows people to organize themselves in order to solve different needs. In the future, more and more needs will be solved this way.

Along with the success of Sales Engineering Finland, I had the idea to write a book on sales skills directed specifically to engineers. At least in Finland, there is no tradition of teaching sales skills to specialists, let alone engineers.

Engineers are taught communication, for example, how to give presentations, but the commercial side of communication is missing: understanding the needs of customers and turning the technical features into benefits for the customers in a way that secures a sale.

Whereas, the traditional sales training is directed to salespeople in general, this book focuses on the sales skills required by an engineer, i.e. a technical specialist; first and foremost on how to sell a technical solution - the substance.

In IT, for example, specialists are nearly always working at the customer interface. They are expected to be able to sell their own work and that of their company, even though a separate salesperson or company management is responsible for commercial deals.

The structure of the book

IMAGE: THE STRUCTURE OF THE BOOK

The structure of this book is based on the modes of persuasion described by Aristotle: **ethos** (credibility), **pathos** (emotion), and **logos** (logical appeal). Together, these three factors make up the backbone of substance selling. These foundations will be discussed from the viewpoint of modern sales and especially of a participating technical specialist. I hope that at least these three tried and tested perspectives on persuasion will remain with you after reading this book.

However, before the selling of the substance can commence, you need to **open the discussion** with the customer in some way. And when you finally agree on cooperation, you must then **negotiate** the deal. These two approaches surround the chapters that focus on selling the substance and they form the sales model described in this book (see the above image). However, first we must discuss how selling has changed and what is the specialist's role in this change.

How to learn by reading?

Top salespeople have a natural talent. It is notoriously difficult to teach what you can do naturally. I myself am not a natural-born seller. For me, an important motivator in writing this book has been to study selling myself. I hope it shows in the text and helps you follow the train of my thoughts. I also believe that my technical background is visible in the text and that I have managed to write about selling in a way that is intelligible to technical specialists.

You cannot learn selling by reading a book. So if you come across an inspiring idea while reading, it is important that you should test it in practice as soon as possible. You learn to sell by doing. Through example and feedback, you can hone your skill and by repetition turn it into a habit and finally into second nature. Reading up too much theory and aiming to gain a perfect understanding of sales may even make it harder to give it a go in practice. Selling is no science. Go ahead and give it a try!

Technical specialist as a salesperson

Salespeople are irritating

When I began to market my book project, I received immediate feedback: "Sounds like bullshit that the shops are full of." This comment speaks volumes about how we view selling.

People often have the wrong impression of what makes a successful salesperson. However, sales is a good field in that rewards come based on results, not style. And there are many styles in which to create results.

According to Finnish customers, the most irritating features of a (bad) salesperson are aggressiveness, indifference towards the customer, and a lack of expertise (Celectus, 2014). I must confess that I used to think these features necessary for sales, and therefore found selling less tempting.

An extrovert is not a good salesperson

Extroverts are viewed as sociable and outgoing. They seek contact with other people and do not find it hard to express their opinions or ask for favors. On the contrary, this energizes them. So it is little wonder that extroverts are often drawn to work in sales. But do they make good salespeople? In our impressions, yes, but not according to studies.

In his book *To Sell is Human: the Surprising Truth About Moving Others*, Daniel Pink presents, perhaps, the most extensive of these studies. The study analyzed three meta-analyses and, altogether, 35 separate studies that had monitored the results of 3,806 salespeople and compared them to the results of personality testing. The correlation between extraversion and delivering results was 0.07, so practically non-existent.

We engineers are easily considered introverted. We like to focus on a few topics that interest us and wish to gain a profound understanding of them. We tend to avoid conflict and consider what we say carefully.

Are introverts good salespeople, then? No. In the study by the renowned social psychologist Adam Grant at The Wharton School of the University of Pennsylvania, introverts reached slightly (though not much) worse results ($120 per hour) than extroverts ($125 per hour).

Grant's study was particularly interesting in that ambiverts, that is people who are at neither end of the personality spectrum (3-5 extraversion on a scale of 1-7), gained a significantly better result than introverts or extroverts ($155 per hour). The best result ($208 per hour) was reached by people directly in the middle (4 on the same scale).

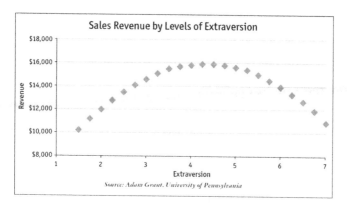

Source: Adam Grant, University of Pennsylvania

IMAGE: STUDY BY THE UNIVERSITY OF PENNSYLVANIA

Since Grant, similar results have been reached in other studies. For example, two studies published by the Harvard Business Review noticed that the most sociable salespeople often performed worst. Contrary to popular belief, excessive extraversion can be a hindrance in selling.

An introvert is prone to understand and an extrovert to suggest. A good salesperson balances these two extremes. They know when to talk, and when to keep quiet. Only a few of us are at either end of this spectrum. So, basically, we are all natural-born sellers.

Selling is not working anymore

Ever since the time of the travelling salesman, the focus of selling has been on making use of the imbalance of information. In the 19th century, when travelling salesmen journeyed from one farm to another presenting their products, the customers had little chance getting to know the experiences of others or compare the products to competing alternatives. However, the salesman created value by spreading information about new products and opportunities.

At the same time, economists have assumed that the market functions efficiently and that buyers make their decisions fully aware of different alternatives. Even though science and education are still to give their full recognition to the value created by selling, it has promoted the spreading of innovation and boosted the operation of the markets ever since the time of the travelling salesman.

The internet has taken the reality of the markets a step closer to the economic theories of perfect competition. The free availability of data has evened out the imbalance of information between sellers and buyers. At the same time, selling and buying have changed. The buyers do not need the seller in the same way as before.

> *"Someone has a car for sale online for ten thousand euros. Then someone else starts to sell a similar car for 9,500 euros and the next one drops the price further. It feels like the customer has become the boss, when it used to be the other way around."*
> *- Timo Tuomi, a car salesman of 35 years in the newspaper Keski-Uusimaa.*

The internet has greatly reduced the traditional role of the seller as a source of information. Customers look up information online on their own initiative. The internet is full of information, guides, and webinars, but also the experiences and opinions of other customers. The customer is often at the end stages of the buying process, if and when they are ready to discuss their issue with a salesperson.

> *"80 percent of B2B buyers find the goods or service supplier they need themselves."*
> *- Aalto University, 2012*

> *"For the first two thirds of the buying process, B2B buyers wish to have no contact with the seller."*
> *- Marketing Clinic, 2012*

Customers are more and more reluctant to meet with salespeople. They feel that the traditional salesperson flogs their own products, asks stupid questions, and provides boring monologues that offer no added value. The modern and busy decision-maker simply does not have time to meet up with vendors without good reason. When all information is readily available online, this reason cannot be the distribution of product information or the presentation of the vendor's offering.

If you went to Starbucks every workday, how long would it take before you had to have the same drink for a second time? The correct answer is 334 years - as Starbucks provides 87,000 different drink combinations.

The number of different alternatives and the amount of information is increasing exponentially, and customers are lost amidst the flood of information, constant change, and mixed messages. They still need a reliable guide with the insight and confidence to help them.

When getting a customer meeting is more difficult than before, the significance of that meeting increases. You cannot afford to waste the rare opportunity. A good salesperson must then be an expert, not only on the products they represent, but on the industry and the customer business as well.

Despite the growing role of the internet in the early stages of the sales process, the salesperson should still be proactive in seeking new opportunities. It is not enough just to be available online for the customer, when they seek a partner for a need they have identified. The salesperson can also create value by helping the customer identify needs that they have not yet thought of. A proactive salesperson always has the upper hand.

As the role of salespeople in the beginning of the buying process diminishes, and the processing of orders can be further automated, what is left for sales is actually what the best salespeople have always done. They are specialists on the customer's business. Now there is less need for repulsive imposing, and selling turns into genuinely helping the customer. This works well for us engineers. Solving problems is what we do.

Creating a customer-specific solution demands expertise. Productization turns a customer-specific solution into a product that can be reproduced and sold to a greater number of clients. It is often thought that this diminishes the need for expertise in selling the productized solution. However, each customer has their own culture, process, and history into which the product must be adapted. This adaptation again demands specialized knowledge.

Productization makes selling easier, but does not remove the need for expertise.

First, convince yourself

When developing your sales skills, remember that the objective is to get the job done, not to do it in a "correct" way. In particular, you should not try to copy that irritating pushy seller people imagine a good salesperson to be like. The most important thing is to be yourself.

We are good at reading other people. If you are not genuine, you will not be trusted, and trust is the most important factor in selling. No one buys what you are selling, they buy what you believe in. It is very hard to sell something in which you have no faith. Enthusiasm is catchy, but so is the lack of it. If you genuinely believe that the customer ought to buy what you are selling, it shows and works. Sales arguments become less important, they come to you naturally.

So you must believe in what you are selling. This requires effort; you must do your homework. You must find the customers to whom or the angle from which you can fully recommend your product. A good salesperson does not sell just anything. So first, you must sell the product to yourself (or your employees).

You must be the best, the cheapest, or the least risky alternative, at least in your own mind and that of your customer. However, you can always change the category within which you are the best option. So you can, or rather you must, differentiate. Take the original Finnish version of this book, for example. The market is full of different guidebooks on sales. Less sales literature is published in Finnish. There are only a couple of guides directed at specialists, and practically nothing for engineers. Although the underlying product is roughly the same, with a small shift in the perspective, I could become a viable option for a Finnish engineer interested in getting started with sales skills.

Often differentiation is not a matter of actual difference, but that of image. For example, shipping companies are willing to pay more to a company that specializes in ship cleaning than to a regular cleaning company, although the work is practically the same. People are also reluctant to change their first impressions. If you are able to be the first to reach a certain position in their minds, the rest seem like copies.

Sales and differentiation are about focusing on the strengths of your own product and looking for a target group to whom these differentiating factors are important. There is no point in denying or developing your weaknesses, unless they directly hinder sales. Selling is not about lying, but about understanding your strengths, finding suitable customers, and solving their needs.

Specialists are particularly needed in the sales of products and services that are valuable and complicated, and often technical, where a great number of people are involved in the decision-making.

The tasks of little added value that are free from selling can increasingly be automated or outsourced. It is often said that the internet will make salespeople redundant, but the truth is the opposite. We will all become salespeople.

Interview: John Care

I had the opportunity to interview John Care, the founder and managing director of Mastering Technical Sales. He is the author of perhaps the best-known book on technical sales, *Mastering Technical Sales: The Sales Engineers Handbook,* and is a globally renowned trainer and speaker. Before becoming a trainer, he led sales support organizations at Oracle, Sybase, Business Objects, Peoplesoft, Nortel, CA Technologies, and HP, among others.

Are engineers needed in sales?

The need for technical specialists in sales organizations is growing rapidly. Globally, there are around 500,000 sales engineers supporting salespeople in technical matters. Clients are more familiar with the market supply than before and demand more expertise from the sales organizations.

IT solutions, in particular, are so complicated, that one person cannot credibly take care of both the commercial and the technical customer relationship. So first and foremost, it is a question of credibility.

In our surveys, at least two thirds of respondents view the technical team as the most valuable part of the supplier's sales organization. Technical specialists understand how products work. They can explain projects conducted for other clients and design innovative solutions, together with specialists from the customer organization. In addition, they are able to explain these solutions to the business management of the customer.

How does an engineer learn to sell?

I learned to sell by observing skilled salespeople and more experienced specialists and by asking a lot of questions. I stole everything that seemed to work. Theory can help you get started, but at some point you simply have to put the ideas into practice. Seek the company of more experienced salespeople and ask them for mentoring.

If you already work in sales, I would recommend asking for feedback from other salespeople, supervisors, and customers. After a meeting, I tend to ask for

- three things I did well

- three things I should not repeat

- three new things I did not do, but ought to try.

You do not have to agree or act on the feedback, but receive the feedback as it is. Do not disagree, and remember to say thank you.

If you are not certain whether you are up to working in sales, try how easy it is for you to translate features into benefits for the customer. Take a feature you have programmed and try to turn it into an advantage and finally into a benefit for the customer or user.

Your tips for engineers?

I believe that being a technical specialist in a sales organization is one of the best jobs there is. You are able to do something that matters and help your customer, while expressing your competitive drive. I can also promise you that the job provides variety; no two weeks are the same. If you do not wish to spend your life in front of a screen, but to work with people, I can warmly recommend switching to sales. Looking forward to having more of us!

Opening the discussion

The bottleneck of sales

"People only buy from you for two reasons. They **know you exist***, and* **they trust you***. Awareness and trust, that's all"*
- Seth Godin

The bottleneck of sales is the opening of new discussions. The old sales formula, according to which result = direction x amount x quality, is still valid. Before a specialist can convince the customer with their expertise, the customer must be aware of their existence.

The more customers you meet, the more you sow the seeds of your message and learn about the customer and the market, even when the discussion leads no further. At the same time, you get valuable practice and hone your message.

Traditionally, the opening of doors and attracting interest has been the task of sales and marketing. Specialists participate in the sales process later and/or ensure the success and growth of existing customers. In a digital world, specialists have a role already at the beginning of the process, for example, as content providers for marketing purposes.

"The future of any company in any industry can be predicted by analyzing the change in the number of new customers. Familiar customers commoditize the business and finally abandon their loyal servant. When they find a better deal, they change suppliers. This is why you must be ready to meet with strangers and spend dangerous minutes on uncharted waters in front of difficult people. Success is about marketing. Its most important bottleneck is in gaining a new customer contact."

- Jari Sarasvuo

Opening a discussion with unknown people is the least favorite section of sales, for specialists in particular. Next, I will go through some modern ways to attract the interest of customers and open discussions that are approachable to specialists and specialized salespeople. Finally, I will also discuss the telephone as a tool. If you want results, you cannot get rid of it.

Inbound marketing

As we have seen, nowadays buyers conduct preliminary research online. Therefore, they expect more and more expertise and vision from the salespeople when they finally contact them. It is important to be present online and guide customers to contact you.

Inbound marketing is a growing marketing strategy, aiming to entice and draw potential customers to contact the seller. Its opposite is the traditional outbound marketing, where the seller approaches potential buyers through selected channels (telemarketing and traditional advertizing, for example).

The objective is to create a digital footprint that reaches customers looking for solutions online and turns them into sales leads. Inbound marketing ties marketing and sales closely together.

Instead of a company's sales process, inbound marketing focuses on the customer's buying process, supporting and guiding it with suitable content. This content should benefit the target group, and not be too selling. Blogs, guides, and other high-quality specialized content aims to gain the customer's trust before the first meeting. If needed, marketing can also be directed to specific customers. This is called account-based marketing.

Inbound marketing utilizes content marketing, which entails the consistent creation and sharing of content. The aim is to attract and engage a specifically defined target group as a customer for the company. Inbound marketing is often executed using marketing automation tools. Marketing automation is an information system which enables the automation of routine communication tasks and the measurement of results.

The inbound marketing process consists of the following stages:

Create content

First, you must understand the customer and their purchase behavior in order to construct suitable content to support the different stages of their purchase process. A common method is to construct fictional customers, buyer personas, to whom the content is directed. The content is then published and potential customers are guided to it via search engines and social media.

The communication of specialists is often plagued by the so-called curse of knowledge. When we understand an issue, we do it so thoroughly that it is hard for us to empathize with the recipient of the message and communicate the issue to a person who does not yet understand it. In their book Made to Stick *Chip and Dan Heath present the simple SUCCESs formula that helps you surpass the curse of knowledge and make your message intelligible and memorable. The formula consists of six parts. The message should be: **S**imple, **U**nexpected, **C**oncrete, **C**redible, **E**motional and **S**tory.*

Convert

The next stage is to recognize those website visitors that are interesting right now. Visitors are usually willing to give their contact details in exchange for valuable content. Not everyone is immediately ready to be contacted, but potential customers need to be engaged and guided forward in the buying process before beginning sales. Interesting customers who are not buying at the moment can be targeted with campaigns that remind them of the company until the time is right.

Measure and develop

Traditionally, it has been difficult to measure achieved results in marketing. However, the entire inbound marketing chain can be measured and repayment can be calculated for all actions. This turns marketing management into engineering, where effective content is discovered through different trials and continuous development and efforts can be directed accordingly.

Social selling

The amount of information available and the ease of finding it have shifted the power from the seller to the buyer. Typically, the customer takes care of preliminary research by themselves before being ready for the seller to join the process. However, the seller naturally wants to join the process as early as possible. One way to achieve this is social selling.

Customers use the internet, especially during the early stages of the buying process. They search and share information, as well as discuss topics, ask questions, and share opinions with friends and strangers. The seller needs to support, help, and serve the customer in solving problems. For this purpose, the seller must be present where the customer is looking for help.

Social selling is about promoting your expertise and offering and building a network through different channels. Social selling creates personal capital that stays with the salesperson fairly well, even when changing jobs.

Today, customers are more reluctant to meet sellers that only promote their own agenda. Instead, they wish to meet salespeople who have something to offer them and from whom they can learn new and useful things.

Social selling does not remove the need for traditional sales tasks, but it facilitates and speeds up the most repulsive stage of selling: the arranging of meetings.

Here are some tips on how to begin social selling:

1. Create profiles to the most important social networks (LinkedIn, Twitter, Facebook).

2. Follow customers, competitors, opinion leaders, and stakeholders.

3. Figure out where content is shared and discussions held in your field (hashtags and Facebook groups, for example).

4. Share interesting and useful content - and not just from your own company. Show leadership, be interested in developing the entire industry. Add value with your own comments, for example.

5. Follow and participate in discussions. Comment, ask, and answer.

6. When needed, open a sales process.

7. Also take care of existing customer relationships and partnerships.

"Focus on helping, not on selling. It is more important to construct your own specialist brand and trust. The more you give of yourself and your expertise online, the more you will receive in the long run. You will be asked for advice and recommendations. People will trust in what you say and share it forward. You may be asked to speak at a seminar or write for a blog. Wouldn't it be nice to be a salesperson, who does not need to call, but who gets calls?"
- AdvanceB2B Social Selling

Social selling has, of course, always taken place, even without social media. Is there even such a thing as asocial selling? The internet is not the only social channel, and the level of its use is also dependent on the sector. The internet has, however, replaced trade fairs as a source of new product information. Even so, professional events, for specialists in particular, are still organized, offering great networking opportunities.

In the best-case scenario, a specialist conducting social selling can gain the customer's trust and help them identify needs, even before the purchase process begins. If all goes well, the customer can skip the time- and energy-consuming search of options and the bidding process and focus on building the best possible solution with the company that has helped them in the beginning. Or, at least, the company has a head start on the competitors.

The fallacy of telemarketing

The death of cold calling has been discussed widely in recent times. Many people, specialists in particular, find cold calling so repulsive that this message is easy to sell.

Some studies suggest that in traditional cold calling only 3% of the contacted are ready to buy and 7% ready to get to know the selling organization. This means that 90% of the contacted are not interested at all. In the light of statistics like these, it is no surprise that many people are not interested in working in sales. However, inbound marketing and social selling emphasize helping the customer and thus attract a completely different kind of people to sales - such as us engineers.

In reality, however, we are far from giving up the active contacting of customers in B2B sales. The role of marketing is emphasized; it is important to be known amongst your customers and available online when a customer looks for a solution for a need they identify. However, the responsibility for initiative still lies with the seller, and the sooner they are included in the buying process, the stronger their position will be when the actual purchase is made.

Instead of mindless pushing, you must focus on finding opportunities to genuinely help the customer and create value. Getting to know the customer, using your expertise and networks, and especially engaging with the customer online will help you recognize these opportunities. The essential thing is to find a good reason for contacting the customer (that is the so-called valid business reason).

An initiative from the customer is not always necessary. You can make up a reason yourself. Once you have come up with a valid reason to call, contacting a customer becomes less repulsive. So, you need to have a reason to contact a particular person or a person in charge of a particular issue. Leave memorized and duplicable sales phrases to the magazine sellers.

Examples:

- Call after a warm inbound marketing lead and ask if you can help.

- Offer value. For example, explain that you could talk about a project you have completed in the same industry.

- Use a reference. "N.N. said that we should talk, because..." is still an effective way to achieve a meeting. Also, remember to ask for recommendations about people you should talk with.

- If you are a significant player on the market, the reason can be as simple as just getting to know each other. It is the buyer's job to monitor, keep up-to-date, and create relationships with central players in the market.

- Ask for feedback on a project your company has completed before.

Remember that the customer assumes that you are aware of their online tracks. Do not start by asking things that you should already know.

You can also contact a customer by using email or social media. For example, turning a contact request into a meeting can usually be done via email. However, the telephone is still an efficient tool in opening a discussion and having a quick dialogue, for example, to find a suitable time for a meeting without sending several emails back and forth.

Ethos - credibility

Nobody cares about what you say

According to studies by Albert Mehrabian, verbal communication has only 7% of impact on what the audience trusts, while the tone of voice has 38%, and the body language 55%. Indeed, it is often said that you must sell yourself first.

In rhetoric, this is called ethos. It is argumentation through trust created by your own personality and reputation. "A person's life persuades better than his word," it was said in Aristotelian times.

Ethos has its roots in biology. Humans and other social animals look up to other group members, especially the leader, on how to behave. Following the individual selected as a leader frees the others from making energy-consuming decisions. Among elephants, for example, decisions are usually made by the most experienced female elephants and others follow their lead.

The correct ethos corresponds with the target group's expectations on the disposition, appearance, and manners suitable for a leader. Ethos is leading by example, it says "do as I say and do". The person who speaks and acts in a way that promotes the objectives valued by the target group has good ethos. But the leader does not need to be one with the audience, but behave as the audience expects a leader to behave.

When speaking to software developers, the suitable ethos is different than when speaking to company management. The old rule of clothing is to dress similarly to the audience - or slightly better. But ethos is not just about clothing or body language.

Elements of trust

According to Aristotle, the following three properties are needed to evoke trust. Here they are discussed in terms of modern sales.

1. Virtue. The customers need to believe that you share their objectives and values.

- Praise yourself. Show that you share the customer's objectives. Be subtle.

- If possible, let someone else give praise to you.

- Reveal a sacrifice or a mistake that confirms you are on the customer's side.

- If needed, change your opinion, based on the customer, even when you think this is not founded. However, avoid the reputation of a turncoat and appeal to new information or perspective, if possible.

    EXAMPLE: You have made a calculation error in a presentation you are going through in a meeting with the customer. You can apologize for the error and explain how you have worked on this important project (emphasis on common objectives) tired overnight (sacrifice), so that this important issue can be concluded on schedule.

2. Practical wisdom. You appear to have the correct answer in any situation.

- Speak of your experiences, share "war stories".

- Show practical wisdom by bending the rules, if needed. Avoid being a wiseass.

- Prefer the middle ground, make the competing presentation seem extreme. People tend to want to avoid extremes.

  EXAMPLE: Propaganda often uses statements that appear ridiculous. The aim is not to get the general public to believe in those statements, but to make people think that the truth lies somewhere between the competitor's propaganda (be it "objective truth") and their own propaganda. The more extreme your claim is towards the direction you wish to take their thoughts, the closer to your position becomes the middle ground in which people tend to trust.

3. Altruism. The customer needs to believe that you are not simply pushing your own case.

- Explain how a conclusion has been unpleasant to you, but inevitable.

- Claim that the decision helps the customer more than in does you, or that it even harms you.

- Express doubts about your own sales skills and commend the skill of your competitors.

   EXAMPLE: "I'm unlikely to get praise for helping you out with this problem, but I am still ready to devote my time to it. The project is just too important to fail."

Trust is not enough

Trust on its own is not enough to convince the customer to take your advice. You must have relevant experience and passion for your substance to be credible.

The correct ethos for a specialized sales representative could be called the trusted advisor. The status of a trusted advisor is not achieved simply through technical expertise. Gaining such a status demands, among other things, keeping your promises, speaking the truth, and acting in the best interests of the customer, even though it may at times be against the best interest of the company you represent.

In his book *The Trusted Advisor Sales Engineer*, John Care defines the trusted advisor with the following formula:

$$\text{TRUSTED ADVISOR FORMULA} = \frac{\text{1. CREDITABILITY} \quad \text{2. RELIABILITY} \quad \text{3. INTIMACY}}{\text{4. SELF-ORIENTATION}} \quad * \text{ 5. POSITIVITY}$$

IMAGE: FORMULA OF A TRUSTED ADVISOR

1. Credibility

Does the customer believe what you say? Do they place value on what you say? Expertise is still at the core, but information and experience alone do not guarantee credibility. In addition to technical information, you must be able to create value for the customer by expressing your technical and/or commercial insight and its benefits to the customer.

- Do not hide unpleasant truths, but remember to be discreet. Do not lie.

- Say if you do not know the answer to a question, find out the answer, and come back to it.

- Express your passion for the product, solution, or service and the industry you represent.

- Make use of your qualifications, certifications, experience, etc. by bringing them up.

- Get to know the company and the people you will meet in advance in order to argue the benefits.

2. Reliability

The customer must learn to rely on you to do what you say.

- Aim for regularity. Chop a big promise into smaller pieces that are easy to keep and exceed.

- Act systematically. Create a clear structure for your activities. I.e. prepare a written agenda and clear goal(s) before the meeting, and write down action points after the meeting.

- Make sure. Write down what you have agreed on and share the information with the client and the rest of the sales team. Ensure that you have correctly understood the essential issues by repeating them verbally.

- Anticipate. In addition to doing what you have promised, anticipate the new needs of the customer.

- Help to prepare. Send material to help the customer prepare for the meeting and support them later.

3. Intimacy

You must understand your customer, both professionally and personally. Several studies have stated that the greatest wish customers place on specialists is that they understand the customer's business, in addition to their own field. This is not enough however, you must also create a relationship with the client as a person -

you must understand their objectives and their way of thinking.

- Be open. Provide information about yourself exceeding your work persona - your hobbies, sports, and children. Find shared interests.

- A shared lunch, dinner, or coffee break is a suitably informal environment for getting to know the customer outside the ongoing work project and learning to read between the lines.

- Be prepared. It is easy to look up information about the customer online and in social media.

4. Self-orientation

Self-orientation acts as a divisor in the formula. Self-orientation reduces your credibility in the eyes of the customer. The more you find yourself thinking about selling, instead of helping the customer, or the next transaction, instead of constructing a customer relationship, the more likely it is that the customer finds you selfish.

Other forms of self-orientation include:

- Interrupting the customer
- Overactivity
- Answering questions too quickly
- Inability to express that you do not know
- Presenting a solution too soon

- Excessive talk of your own technology and company

- Listening in order to reply, not to understand

- Hogging information, not helping your colleagues.

You can develop your behavior:

- Ask what the customer thinks about a situation, suggestion, etc.

- Listen, pause before you answer.

- Do not present a solution too soon. Let the customer express their views.

- Take responsibility for communication problems or when something goes wrong.

- Do the right thing. Do not be right.

5. Positivity

Positivity does not mean that you should keep smiling and be naively confident that everything will work out. Positivity is about focusing more on the opportunities than on the challenges. Positivity is a can-do attitude. But it must be genuine, true to your style.

- Be confident. Customers and sellers do not like uncertainty, as it increases the sense of risk.

- Be optimistic. Hold on to realism, but also look for opportunities.

- Respect others and give thanks for their help. Speak good things about others behind their backs, not bad.

- Say "yes and" instead of

- "yes, but". This is an old exercise from improvisational theatre, creating a positive, open cycle to the discussion

- Practice. The human mind is prone to focus on things that could go wrong. Make the effort to go through the positive things that could happen.

Serve in advance and for free

As we have learned, the customer must trust you to act in their best interest. This trust must be built before they are ready to share their issues. Without it, you cannot reach the core of their problems and offer your solutions.

As a specialist, you already have a better starting point than a salesperson. Generally speaking, customers share their problems more openly with a specialist than with a salesperson.

The company brand also supports you in building trust, but you must deliver on its promise: meet the customer's expectations or even exceed them.

Trust building takes place by serving and helping the customer before the actual selling begins. This is done in small sections, little by little.

The entire sales process and every meeting must create value. The customer does not wish to meet simply to explain their situation. Neither should you meet the customer simply to speak about your products.

The commitment between a customer and a seller should grow hand in hand, at the same pace. If one party invests more (time, money, risk) in the relationship, the other will automatically begin to take advantage.

Nowadays, trust building often starts online. When before, the building of trust required several meetings, now the customer may be willing to buy quickly, if the trust has been built beforehand.

Interview: Sani Leino

Sani Leino is an energetic trainer in the areas of sales, customer experience, and digital interaction. Sani has over 10 years of experience in result-driven B2B sales, especially in the ICT, Telecom, and Retail sectors. Over the past ten years, Sani has worked for companies, such as Toyota, Gigantti, DNA, and the sales company Celectus in various tasks in sales. Currently, Sani works as the European Sales Director of technology company ThingLink with responsibility for B2B sales, the development of an international partner program, and the construction of a retailer network.

How has selling changed?

The traditional basic principles of sales have not changed at all, but we are now truly living in the era of the powerful customer. It puts pressure on changing our operation models towards more customer-oriented sales. We still need strong interaction skills, the ability for active listening and an argumentation of solutions, as well as emotional intelligence and discretion. In the world of the internet and the enormous number of alternatives, the customer genuinely has all options available, which puts pressure on the sales organization to provide value at an earlier stage, that is, when the customer is still looking for suitable supplier candidates from a number of alternatives.

Increasingly, the buying process begins online and the customer needs are not necessarily defined and charted face-to-face. This is why the seller must be able to respond as early as possible to the need definition and value creation.

The modern salesperson should shift from reactive value creation towards proactive value creation. Salespeople should make use of technology and new types of channels in a new way. We need to use the same channels our customers use. We must make full use of online content that makes it easier for the customer to find information and define their true needs.

We salespeople must also be better prepared for a meeting with the customer. We must produce value at an earlier stage and thus create a real need for a face-to-face meeting. With a genuine need and a clearly defined agenda, the mutual expected value for the meeting is high. This way, both the salesperson and the customer will feel that the meeting was sensible, necessary, and efficient.

The internet was rumored to eliminate the salesperson, but it now appears as an excellent solution for them, if used right. It allows them to offer valuable help at an earlier stage to more and more customers lost within a flood of information and unlimited alternatives.

Why is expertise the key?

As everything is visible and transparent online, unfounded claims do not tend to work. The customer's trust needs to be earned. This becomes easier when the seller already creates value at the enquiry stage. This makes the customer interested in the seller as a specialist, instead of a traditional salesperson.

The advantage of the more transparent digital era is that the status of a specialist is more and more defined through contents, connections, and competences. It is easier for different specialists to promote their competence, whereas earlier this has been challenging due to the bigger players taking over the airspace with money and market share.

In the digital era, actions and competence speak louder than titles. Now, many specialists have a better opportunity to influence online in both domestic and foreign markets with their clever content and views. This was not necessarily possible before.

The style of content and communication should in my opinion be as genuine and human as possible. Robotic and corporate mass information does not work in channels where the main value comes from authenticity and the reliability of information.

Is cold calling dead?

Cold calling is not dead, but an extremely inefficient method of attracting new customers in certain sectors. Therefore, many have become frustrated and wondered how to better reach future customer candidates.

In Finland, for example, cold calling is still reasonably effective in general, but here as well the trend is towards more personalized communication methods.

I wish to emphasize that calling or the telephone as a tool in general have not gone anywhere and are likely to remain as the primary tool of a salesperson for many years to come. However, the tool kit of the salesperson will include other channels aiming to influence a growing group of customer representatives included in decision-making. The latest studies (CEB 2016) show that an average B2B decision-making process may include more than 6 people, so the salesperson alone is rarely capable of impacting the entire buying process.

Your tips for engineers?

1. Share your expertise openly

Understand that the customers increasingly begin their purchase process online. To be able to influence the deliberation period and the actual transaction phase, you must also be present when the customer looks for information. Find and test the best environments and operation models in your sector on how to produce content or make your expertise visible. Construct your specialist brand in the long term. Why? Because specialists are shown to be thought of as more reliable sources of information than company management (the annual Edelman Trust Barometer).

2. Understand your excellence

It could be said that engineers, if anyone, are specialists and thus also highly trusted advisers. In a study describing the Finnish salesperson (Taloustutkimus 2014), by far the most valued characteristic of a salesperson was expertise.

So when a Finnish buyer approaches a salesperson, they expect insight and expertise. This should be perfectly suited for engineers.

The second most important characteristic was the willingness to serve, which can be easily learned when you understand that the customer has an unlimited amount of options available. Our task as modern salespeople is to help customers in their buying process in a way that is valuable to them.

3. Understand the importance of emotional intelligence

Although the number of channels and handy tools is increasing dramatically, we must remember that, ultimately, the customer is not interested in channels or tools. The customer is looking for benefits for their business or help with their problems - the tools or technologies the seller uses to solve the customer's problems come second.

The fundamental purpose of technological tools in sales is the development of the seller's operation on one hand, and the better understanding of the customer and their business on the other. In addition to different digital skills, it is very important to understand and remember the importance of emotional skills, as well. No technology or channel will replace face-to-face meetings, nor is that their purpose.

Digital channels and tools emphasize the importance of a face-to-face meeting, when we know more about each other and our needs. When we finally meet up with the customer, the significance of emotional intelligence is crucial to the actual purchase decision.

Without proper digital skills, the seller finds it hard to identify the actual need of the customer and this can dilute value creation in the meeting. But without emotional skills, the salesperson can have meeting after meeting while not creating genuine value to the customer. This will end many a relationship before they start.

The modern salesperson understands the importance of digital and social channels in identifying sales opportunities. They know what is needed for starting a discussion and understand the importance of emotional intelligence in building trust and creating a customer relationship.

Pathos - emotion

Maybe decisions
are not made with the heart?

You must have heard the claim that a purchase decision is made with the heart and explained afterwards with the head. Is it so?

The oldest part of our brain is the so-called limbic system that participates in the regulation of autonomic processes, motivation, and emotions. The limbic system is tightly connected to the memory and the senses, but it does not understand language or logic. These are located in the cerebral cortex that developed more recently. The logical and linguistic system is subordinated to the older limbic system. Our understanding is created in the cerebral cortex, but words receive their meaning through the limbic system. MRI scans of the brain show that, regardless of the person, the limbic system always activates before the cerebral cortex.

Does this mean that we always make decisions guided by emotion? Not necessarily. According to a well-known example, the relationship between the conscious mind and emotions can be compared to a mouse riding an elephant. If the elephant remains calm, the small mouse on its back can guide it to the desired direction. But if the elephant bolts, the mouse might as well give up.

This is what makes trust so important. If we achieve trust and an emotional connection with our customers, we are then able to persuade them through logical argumentation. Our emotional system is constantly observing our surroundings and risks within it. For evolutionary reasons, the easiest way to calm down the customer is to find something you have in common; show that you belong to the same tribe. A particularly strong connection can be created through finding a shared enemy. A common enemy, if anything, will prove you are part of the same tribe. This connection does not need to be particularly logical in terms of other cooperation. That you both like craft beer can be enough to create the necessary trust for selling technology.

An emotional connection creates trust, but distance contributes to authority. Many professional groups (such as doctors) deliberately keep their distance from their clients to maintain authority - we are naturally prone to obey authorities.

The most significant emotion preventing a sales deal is that of risk. Mixed emotions, in particular, can make the decision-making more difficult and lead to dithering. However, contradictions make people more receptive to alternative views and can be used to make the other party change their mind.

Generally speaking, people are more afraid of losing than gaining something. In order to finalize a sales deal, you should evoke the feeling that missing out on the deal is a greater loss than making it.

Finalizing a sales deal often requires the feeling that the customer will lose something, if they do not make the deal right now (for example, a limited offer).

How to create emotions?

So emotions are primary, compared to thinking. You can sooth emotions and talk sense, but emotions also offer you a backdoor through which you can access the unconscious mind and impact your customer's thinking.

"An old James Bond movie is showing on the screen in a dark seminar hall, actually it's the very first one, Doctor No. Sean Connery is lying under silk sheets. Suddenly he startles. There is fear on his face. He starts to recede slowly. I do the same in my chair. And the person next to me does the same. A large black tarantula climbs up the secret agent's arm." This description of a journalist's reaction comes from an article on mirror neurons in *Tiede* science magazine (1 November 2005).

Mirror neurons provide the basis for empathy. They recognize sounds, facial expressions, and gestures, mirror them in our brains, and then let us know what others are doing and experiencing. In the example above, the journalist mirrored James Bond's expressions and gestures, and when the information reached the emergency center of the brain, the amygdalae, he experienced the fright that the tarantula gave the secret agent.

When we see an angry person, we get angry. When we see a sad person, we get sad. We do not consciously recognize this reaction, because it takes place at the limbic system level. The transfer of emotions is a deeply human phenomenon and it is nearly impossible to defend against it.

Our emotions are mirrored, especially when we are new to a situation. People turn to look at the newcomer and mirror that person's emotions. Individuals in leading positions are mirrored more closely than others. In general, our emotions are mirrored more than we think. Take public speaking, for example. If you are nervous and focused on yourself, the audience will focus on themselves as well. If you are enthusiastic and focused on the audience, the audience will focus on you.

If you wish to create some emotion for others, you must first feel it yourself. For example, get to know method acting techniques that are used to achieve a certain emotional state. However, more important than creating an emotion is to openly show your emotional state and not to hide your feelings.

In sales, it is good to be (self-)confident about your case. Confidence is catchy; the customer feels they can trust you and this reduces the feeling of risk. You can develop your self-confidence. The construction of self-confidence is based on repeated successes. Whatever your target, first set your bar low enough and then slowly raise it to gain a repeated experience of success. This increases confidence in your own operation.

Modern information work is not very concrete and targets are often rather vague. This can make it unclear whether you have succeeded in your work. Help comes from setting concrete targets, for example, for what you should achieve each week. Writing down these targets and monitoring them makes work more concrete and defined. With clear targets, you can feel you have succeeded.

It is also worth remembering that the mind lives in the body. In addition to fitness, physical posture can affect self-confidence. A few minutes standing in the so-called superman pose - legs wide, chin up and chest pushed forward, shoulders back and hands on the waist - is visible as increased testosterone levels. See Amy Cuddy's TED talk *Your body language shapes who you are.*

Story, a backdoor to the mind

When you imagine doing something, your brain activates as it does when actually doing the thing. This is what makes stories so powerful. The key thing is that the listener identifies with the main character and lives the emotions experienced by that person through them.

A story is a method of transferring an experience from one person to another. Stories have had a central role in human evolution. Stories have allowed evolution to make a break from genes and move to cultural evolution. People have used stories to share their experiences on how to behave in different situations. People particularly remember stories that include a threatening situation or tension, because remembering such events has been useful for survival.

According to narrative psychology, stories are a human method of thinking, observing, imagining, and making decisions. Our mind is constantly observing our surroundings and, based on our previous experiences, aiming to recognize stimuli and predict how to react to them. So we only pay attention to stimuli that are significant, based on our earlier experiences. We do not see reality as it is, but we interpret it through our experiences (or stories we have heard).

Some philosophers view consciousness as an emotion created by this story machine in our brain of knowing what will happen next. When we meditate, for example, we are fully present in the moment, and lose consciousness. So we may be able to modify the core of a person, their consciousness/identity, through a backdoor.

Our brain uses stories to predict the future, based on past experiences. In a rapidly evolving world, development requires unlearning, as old experiences no longer offer us the correct vision of the future.

Classical rhetoric teaches us that when talking about the past, we look to place guilt, when talking about the present, we emphasize values, give praise or criticism, and construct unity or separation, and when talking about the future, we discuss options and choices.

Moving the discussion to the future reduces conflicts and builds cooperation.

It is said that without first-hand experience, a concept is empty. Experiences and their form transferrable from one person to another, stories, give words their meaning. A clever negotiator does not debate using logic, but plays with values and meanings. A logical engineer, at least, is easy to baffle by playing with the meaning of words instead of the words themselves.

The three main ingredients of a good story are identification, tension, and resolution. Without them, a story does not work. First, the listener must emphasize with the story through a character as if it was happening to them. Without tension, our brains will not receive the story, as it is not significant from an evolutionary point of view. And lastly, without resolution the story is left open and the listener does not get their gratification.

A common sin of specialists is to spew out everything they know to the tiniest detail and answer questions that have not been asked. The customer finds it hard to receive an unstructured and often abstract flood of information, and this only results in an increased feeling of risk.

Stories are a great method of giving a concrete example of what the issue could mean to the customer. The tension in the story explains the problem we wish to solve. A story constructed this way appeals to our emotions and creates a deeper meaning for our solution.

The story can be constructed according to the following basic formula by Gustav Freytag:

1. **Exposition,** introduces the starting position and different parties.

2. **Rising action,** the change that begins to build tension.

3. **Climax,** where the main character concretely understands the severity of the situation.

4. **Falling action,** where the tension is fought.

5. **Resolution,** where a new balance is found.

Reference stories, in particular, work, as they speak of how a party similar to your customer solved a challenge with your help. The reference follows the basic story formula and makes use of the principle of social proof that states that when we are insecure we want to see what others like us are doing. If we then consciously did differently than others and it went belly-up, we would have a hard time explaining it to our boss.

Another advantage of stories is that you cannot argue against them. A story turns the general into personal, the abstract into concrete, and the theoretical into emotion. A story describes one experience and cannot be denied. "A story distributes beliefs, but does not care whether they are true or not," says Juhana Torkki in his book *Tarinan valta*.

Juhana Torkki summarizes the telling of a good story to the following tips:

1. In the message content, concentrate on what appeals to the emotions, i.e. is meaningful.

2. Present solutions for concrete problems.

3. Construct the Aristotelian drama structure, according to Gustav Freytag's model.

4. Use archetypes, universal story forms that appeal strongly to people. You can steal them from movies, stories or myths, etc.

5. Build a role for your listeners, so that they can continue the story with their actions (for example, they can identify with the hero that saves the IT department with your product).

When NO comes out of nowhere

Even when you have used faultless argumentation to convince the customer of the excellence of your solution, the end result may be the following:

- You: Do you like the idea? The customer: Yes. It seems really interesting.

- You: Do you think it would lead you forward? The customer: Definitely. We need it.

- You: Is our price level correct? The customer: Yes. You are competitive.

- You: So, what do you say, should we start cooperation? The customer: We need to think about it.

Here you have not achieved an emotional connection with the customer and their sense of risk is preventing them from making a decision. If this situation seems familiar, you must pay more attention to the building of trust and emotional appeal of your proposal.

Interview: John Bates

John Bates is a world-renowned presentational speaking coach. He has trained the management, for example, at Johnson & Johnson, Accenture, NASA, IBM, and Boston Scientific to be better performers. John has also trained hundreds of TED and TEDx speakers and written the book *World Class Speaking in Action*. He has held the role of Chief Evangelist in the following technology companies: Virtual Vegas, BigWords.com, MindArk, and Goldstar.com.

What is the role of emotions?

I basically feel that the only way to truly make people do something, like sign a contract or make a purchase, is to appeal to the emotional section of the brain. My world changed when I realized that we all think we live in our conscious mind, but this is not true. Our conscious mind is subordinated to the lower sections of the brain.

Even the thinking of the most logical of engineers can be shown to be based on emotions in an MRI scan. When the engineer is to make a decision, we can see that the sections of the brain that handle emotions react prior to the frontal lobe where thinking takes place.

Affecting the emotions is not as complicated as we may think. For me, it means calming down the emotional part of the brain. In practice, this requires an emotional connection that is created when we find a common denominator that lets us feel part of the same tribe. This connection is based on emotions and does not need to be in any way sensible. If we both like dogs, for example, this can create trust for other cooperation, as well.

We all have mirror neurons that let us experience empathy. They let us feel what we see others feeling. These neurons function unconsciously and very effectively. It is nearly impossible to avoid emotions being transferred. We constantly monitor the emotions of others. Therefore, it is important to recognize the emotional state we are giving out. If you are nervous, your customer feels it. Nervous people do not sign contracts.

How to tell a good story?

Stories have been a way to share knowledge throughout human history. Stories have been so integral to evolution that if our ancestors had not been good at telling stories, we would not exist.

So fundamentally, we are all good storytellers. Still we find it hard and feel that only authors or Hollywood scriptwriters can tell good stories. This is not true, anyone can tell a story.

I have noticed that the most important realization in becoming a better storyteller is to tell the story from the audience's point of view, not from your own. Tell the story to the audience, not to yourself.

In practice, this means not telling the whole story. Leave out details that mean nothing to your audience. It is also worth thinking about where to start the story and how to make it fun, instead of just telling the facts.

This often means starting at some exciting point in the middle of the story, and then returning to how the story got there and taking the audience to the climax.

Also come up with a way to add something funny and surprising to your story. With a little effort, your story becomes so good that you become absorbed in it as well.

Your tips for engineers?

I value the technical specialists' commitment to logical thinking. However, if they wish to achieve even more, they should remember that logic and emotion are like two pedals on a bicycle. You can peddle as hard as you like on the logical side, but if you don't implement emotion, the bicycle is going nowhere. If you want to be a good communicator, you must learn to loosen your tight logical grip when needed.

It can be scary to show emotion. A poker face comes handy in many situations, but when you wish to sell something or lead people, it is of no use. I believe that it is brave and generous to let people see your feelings. If you wish to succeed with people, you must utilize your emotions.

An exercise I have tried with highly logical managers, for example, at organizations such as NASA and Accenture, is to make them read children's stories aloud. This has made them realize how much fun showing your emotions can be and they have been able to take the experience with them to the corporate setting.

These exercises work as they help you forget self-criticism, which is at the core of my teaching. Stop thinking about yourself and think of your audience. Let them feel they are ok. This makes everything much easier.

Logos - argumentation

You are selling the wrong thing

Do not sell the product, but the problem it solves.

Due to our background in mathematics and natural sciences, we engineers are strong in logic. We tend to trust the logical argument in sales, as well.

In the previous chapters, we have learned that without trust and an emotional connection, even the best of arguments fall on deaf ears. Trust and a suitable emotional connection provide the foundation for making a sale, but a well-structured and founded sales argument is still a prerequisite for sales.

The natural argumentation of engineers has its own pitfalls, the greatest being the lack of customer-orientation. Engineers often seem to think that the salesperson's task is to sell the company's products. However in principle, the customer is not interested in the offering of the seller, but their own needs. The salesperson should primarily sell **the need that can be solved** competitively with their **product**. Need, solution, product. In this order.

The need can be hidden or vague and require clarification. A good salesperson has a profound understanding of the customer business and can help the customer identify this need. However, the need comes from the customer. The salesperson does not bring it from outside. Naturally, the ever-changing world also creates new needs: technology in the industry develops, new legislation demands action, structures change and so forth.

In his blog, Jari Parantainen points out that the problem for engineers in particular is trying to solve problems that do not exist:

"Far too often, an entrepreneur has somehow got the idea that their task in life is to create a completely new product or service category. Engineers, in particular, are keen to use their logical-rational world view to create products that are of no interest to anyone. Sadly, converting and public education is insanely expensive. Without force, only a few organizations in the world are able to do this. Even Google must often state that its wooing power was not enough to create a "new need".

In the traditional sales model, the existing need and relevant authority is ensured by asking straightforward questions, according to the classic BANT model (budget, authority, need, timeframe). This assumes that the customer has identified the need, has the authority to make relevant decisions, and wishes to meet with the seller to gain further information.

The traditional sales meeting is easily focused on the presentation of the **product** and understanding the customer need and finding a relevant solution get sidetracked.

With all information available online, the salesperson acting according to the traditional model provides little added value as a provider of new information. Product information is now online and the power lies with the customer. The customer has usually identified a need and began to compare different solutions before being ready to meet with a seller.

With the unlimited offering of suppliers, information, and opinions available online, the customer looks to the salesperson, not for product presentations, but for support and insight in clarifying and solving their **needs** and making a decision.

The most common reasons why a customer dislikes the salesperson (Kelley Robertson 2008):

1. The salesperson does not listen.

2. The salesperson talks too much.

3. Lack of knowledge.

Engineer logic is not working

Let us return to argumentation. You have gained the customer's trust and they want to hear your views on their situation. The customer expects that you understand their need and wish to solve it. Your argumentation must be based on the reality experienced by the customer. If the customer does not believe in the premise, the bottom falls out of your argumentation.

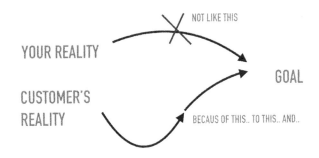

FIGURE: YOU DO NOT NEED TO SHOW THAT THE CUSTOMER IS WRONG. ACCEPT THEIR REALITY AND CONSTRUCT YOUR ARGUMENT FROM IT.

In sales argumentation, it is not essential whether the customer is right or not, but how you can construct an argumentation chain between the reality they are experiencing and the solution you are suggesting. The first task is to sell a shared understanding of the need and then build your story on top.

Engineers tend to think that there is a shared empirically proven foundation, based on which conclusions can be made. This may apply in natural sciences, but in a sales situation easily leads you to present your own great idea missing the reality of the customer. Instead, you should understand the customer needs and speak of them in a language the customer understands.

A need is rarely sold to one person. Often it is a matter of selling a consensus to an entire organization. The customer's problems are often caused by silos and/or part optimization past which no single unit can see. By networking across these silos, the salesperson can help the customer's management identify a need that no single silo representative brings up.

There is no use in pushing your own conclusions down the opposite party's throat. This only results in a defensive reaction. Challenging the customer means opening up new perspectives, not showing that they are wrong. Entice the customer with small baits to leap from their position towards your objective. Let them figure out the issue themselves. We are all more committed to ideas we come up with ourselves (Not Invented Here).

Getting to the core

The customer has done their background work and knows your company and solution on some level. They expect the same from you. They have probably left some kinds of tracks online and expect you to be generally aware of their situation. There is no need for long foreplay. You can get straight to the point.

In modern sales, value is created through dialogue between the seller and the customer. It is a matter of sparring more than straightforward solving of the customer's problem. The collision of different views and experiences creates new insights; needs and their solutions. This is the core of sales and it is going nowhere.

Discussion is opened up through open questions. HubSpot has developed a replacement for the traditional BANT model described earlier. The starting point of their question model GPCT (Goals, Plans, Challenges, Timeline) A (Authority) C&I (Negative Consequences and Positive Implications) is that the customer has already identified a need and began to chart their options. It aims to deepen the understanding of the customer's situation and, at the same time, create value to the customer.

1. **Goals:** What are the goals of the company/unit? The salesperson can create value by helping to make concrete what the higher objectives mean for everyday work or what kind of intermediary goals they demand.

2. **Plans:** How is the customer planning to achieve their goals? Have they tried the same before and has it worked? The salesperson can create value by speaking of how other customers have tried to solve the same problem.

3. **Challenges:** What is stopping them from reaching the goals? You can express your views of future challenges. Without a current or anticipated challenge, the customer is not ready to change their plans. You can ask: Do you believe you have the sufficient expertise to solve this problem?

4. **Timeline:** When must the targets be met? When can the customer execute their plans? When does the customer want to solve the problem? Do you find the timeframe realistic? If the answer is "in the future", it is worth considering how much time you should spend on the customer.

5. **Budget:** The customer cannot buy without a budget. So figure out whether they are able to invest in your solution. You can ask this directly and evaluate whether it is realistic or help with prioritization. Maybe funds can be transferred to you from somewhere else? Generally only those with no budget skirt around the answer. Often people just want to chat with specialists, in particular.

6. **Authority:** Usually the person guarding the money chest is not the one who finds out about different solution alternatives. So remember that the actual decision-maker tends to be behind the person you are talking to. That person is your actual customer and you must help the middle-man sell your solution to them. Always try to meet with the actual decision-maker and understand their situation (using the same model).

7. **Consequences:** What will happen when the customer meets the targets (also personally)? Does not reach them? Is late? By coming up with negative consequences and positive implications, you can help the customer understand risks and opportunities. Here you can add pressure and direct the conversation towards your solution.

The counterpart to asking is listening. Listen in order to understand, not to respond. The customer must feel that they are understood and that you are interested in their needs. This demands active listening. This can include:

- Nodding, understanding facial expressions and suitably timed mumbling.

- Repeating in your own words: Did I understand correctly...? You can reform and direct the conversation at the same time.

- Follow-up and specifying questions: What would this mean to you personally?

- Also remember to take a break before complementing the customer's answer with our own views. Otherwise, it creates the impression that you have not been listening.

From technology to the need

Discussion has now let you grasp the customer reality and needs, based on which you should build your argument or presentation. The FAB model helps in constructing the presentation content.

- **What (feature)** - explains the properties of the product. For example, a gym: five exercise bikes, modern sauna facilities, 24/7 solarium. It is also important to state clearly what you are selling, at least in a contract.

- **How (advantage)** - explains the **solution** enabled by the properties. The gym: bigger muscles, better aerobic fitness, weight loss. This explains the **change** or difference to competitors.

- **Why (benefit)** - explains the **benefits** brought by the solution. Why answers to the **need**. The gym: more sex or better health.

Specialists, in particular, often seek new information for new information's sake. When a specialist is very interested in how something works, you may be wasting your time. They may not have a real project behind them with objectives, schedules, and a budget.

Decision-makers are more interested in benefits, costs, and risks than how they are achieved. Generally you must design your presentation for the decision-maker, even when you are not directly presenting to that person. Ultimately you are supporting your customer in providing a report to the decision-maker. Here they might need your help.

1. Repeat the problem or need (why)

The thing we people fear most is loss. You should sell the belief that not solving the problem now is the greatest loss. Add pressure by repeating the consequences that the unsolved issue is currently causing. The need may sometimes feel self-evident, but it is always good to warm up the recipient by recalling the problem clearly and, at the same time, ensuring that you have a shared understanding of that need. Be concrete and repeat what the problem specifically means to the recipient personally and on an organizational level.

2. Describe the solution (how)

Share your views on how the needed change can be achieved, what options are available to the customer, and what parts and stages make up the solution. Show that you understand the whole, even when you can only offer a section of it. You can present different approaches and compare them with each other. You are not yet selling your own product, but helping the customer as an "independent" consultant. You can, of course, explain the benefits of your approach and differences to competitors, but the focus is still on the approach or concept, not on the product.

3. Explain your offering (what)

Explain what part of the whole you can offer and how you have packaged it. Remember that the decision-maker is interested in benefits, risks, and costs. Repeat why you, your company, and your product would be the best partner for the customer. Present references to diminish the feeling of risk.

Preparation is everything in giving a presentation. You must know your audience and your targets. If you give the same presentation more than once, you'll notice how it improves each time and you can anticipate the reactions and questions of the listener. This is also why you should practice the presentation at least a couple of times before giving it.

4. Take the initiative

Make it easy to buy and take initiative of the next step. Say how you could move forward. Do not suggest a too large whole, but the first small and concrete step that is easy to take, if they have bought your story thus far.

Beg for objections

Questions and objections are a good thing. They let the customer show what troubles them or is important to them. Objections offer the opportunity to learn, correct misunderstandings, and eliminate obstacles. So encourage the customer to express their views. Do not argue back or imagine that you know the customer's situation better than they do.

Usually the same questions appear from one customer to the next. You have the upper hand, as most likely you have discussed the same topic with many other customers. Different customers ask the same questions and you will quickly learn the suitable answers for the most common ones.

Objections could be classified, as follows:

> **Well-founded objection:** A well-founded objection is the best you can wish for. You simply have to remove the reasonable obstacle, and the deal is yours.

> **Opponent:** A weakness brought up by someone who opposes your solution. You have probably answered this before. Remember to stick to your strengths, refuse to comment on competitors.

Guru: If the customer asks for irrelevant things or details for intellectual interest, give brief answers and point them to additional material, in order to move forward.

Fan: If the customer asks a question simply to bring out your strengths, listen to them and answer naturally, as you would any other question.

Attacker: If the customer behaves inappropriately and starts to question your presentation or expertise, keep your calm. You can slow down to calm the situation and offer to discuss the matter afterwards.

Generic objection: Not an objection as such, but an expression of unwillingness or inability to make the decision. For example: "Your solution is too expensive".

The following is a general model for dealing with objections:

1. **Listen** carefully. Show that you respect the opinion and someone else may respond for you.

2. **Coordinate**, who answers for what.

3. **Clarify**, request specification. Disregard an irrelevant question by asking for an example on how this affects their case. Or ask for reasons for the question. This may allow you to solve the issue differently by moving from the feature request towards the true need.

4. **Repeat** the question in order to show that you have understood it. You can also formulate the phrases for your own benefit.

5. **Give** the answer in a concise way (if the answer is long, start by saying yes or no). If you do not know, admit it and say that you will find out. A drawing may help in summarizing the issue. Confirm that the issue is understood.

Ultimately, the most important thing is...

Finally, it is important to remember that you must own your case. Tell the customer that you will personally take care of reaching the agreed target. You only need their blessing to move forward and you will take care of the rest.

The salesperson must be proactive: "If you do not have an agenda, you are a part of someone else's agenda". Show how you could proceed. But do not ask for too much at a time. Proof of Concept or its design meeting may be enough to sell at one time. Define your targets before the meeting.

If the customer needs to make an effort to move your case forward, it will not happen. If you start asking the customer for reports on the progress of your project, you will soon be talking to an answering machine.

Ask who you should work with and do the work for the customer. This allows you to suggest the next steps, as well. You are interesting, when you get things done and the customer can focus elsewhere.

Take the initiative. Do the job. Own the next step.

Interview: Timo Sorri

Timo Sorri is a Presentation Designer and the founder and CEO of Havain Oy. He has a Master of Science (Technology) degree and effective sales presentations are his passion. Timo's background is in IT management consulting, marketing, and sales. Now he helps his customers - both small businesses and global groups and public administration bodies - to communicate their ideas in a selling, clear and convincing manner and to create automated marketing campaigns.

What is a good sales presentation like?

The best sales presentation does not feel like a presentation. It feels like a coaching discussion between a customer and a specialist. Nowadays, information about different solutions is widely available online and social networks readily answer any question. The customer usually assumes that they can study the basic data of a product or service online. In this case, the sales presentation must provide added value by helping the customer figure out a way forward from their current situation and by adapting the solution to the customer's reality.

A good sales presentation therefore supports the forming of a shared understanding through discussion.

Instead of listing the product and supplier company information, I would suggest constructing the sales presentation around the following questions:

> **What is the customer's problem?** (interest and a shared understanding of the reality of the situation)
>
> **Why should they quickly tackle the problem and make a change to the situation?** (fear of loss)
>
> **What is the solution and its benefits?** (possibility of gain)
>
> **How to reach the solution?** (initiative on the next step)

The weakness of engineers?

Excessive faith in that the product will sell itself. The salesperson's task is to:

1. build a relationship of trust between the customer and the selling organization

2. inspire the customer to specifically select the salesperson's solution

3. guide the customer confidently towards a decision by taking the initiative.

All of these can be included in a formal sales presentation (PowerPoint, for example), but a good salesperson adapts their presentation to correspond with the situation of the customer.

What is the best way to develop?

The best way to develop one's skills is to take part in sales meetings and gain experience and vision through them. If an engineer wishes to practice their body language, I would recommend Toastmasters public speaking clubs. They allow you to practice in a safe and encouraging environment.

Your tips for engineers?

Learn to use body language (intonation, gestures, movements) to liven up your performance. In my opinion, the main issue for engineers is not in evoking trust or managing the sales process, but in standing out from the crowd and generating enthusiasm for their product. By using body language, you can show how excited you are about the product you offer, and then spread that enthusiasm.

Negotiation skills

Let the match begin

Once, we were designing a national online service for our client. The underlying system was based on technology that had user-specific licenses. The service had previously had a few dozen users. The first offer from the technology supplier for a license of five million users (the population of Finland) was 2,000,000,000 euros. We presented them with an alternative solution, replacing their technology with another with realistic costs of around 200,000 euros. So we finally reached a win-win solution, where the supplier provided the customer with a 99.9999% discount.

The technical specialist has usually taken care of their share of the sales process, when commercial negotiations begin. It is often emphasized that the specialist should avoid discussing topics that can effect the negotiation, unless separately agreed upon with the person in charge of the commercial negotiation.

The specialist may reveal, for instance, that changes to some technical connection can usually be done with no extra charge. Even though this may be true and the cost of such changes is insignificant, the tiniest concession may have a great impact when negotiating the whole.

So it is best for the specialist to avoid commenting on questions outside their area of responsibility. It is worth having an answer ready for situations where you have to avoid a commercial question. For example: "Unfortunately, I am unable to comment on how this affects the entire project under discussion. You'll have to take it up with the salesperson in charge of your account," usually works well.

When technical specialists are included in sales, it is usually a question of complex solutions with wide implications for the customer's operation. Specialists are needed to adapt the solution on sale to the situation of the customer, that is, existing infrastructure, processes, and culture. The decision of the customer is usually made by more than one person. The process can include a wide variety of representatives and specialists from different operations.

Decision-making is generally a political process, where the customer may have several interest groups with different agendas. The technical specialist supporting or taking care of sales must develop their understanding of power struggles and negotiation forces in order to succeed in such a complex environment.

Life is a negotiation

Negotiation skills are not only needed in commercial negotiations. You are not always able to direct negotiations to the salesperson in charge of the commercial relationship. For example, the customer may validly demand that the product or service you represent should be tested in their environment before they can consider moving forward. This leads to a negotiation situation in which you will most likely take part. Does the testing cost? How is success evaluated? What does the customer commit to, if the test is a success?

I am often asked to present new versions and properties of our products to customers. And often I agree to do so. I give my presentation, leave, and gain practically nothing from the meeting. In this everyday negotiation situation, I could ask the customer to tell me more about their situation, needs, and plans in exchange. This would benefit us both, as it would help me adapt our presentation to meet their needs.

Power and negotiation are included in all interaction. Most agreements are not written down or even said out loud. Usually, an agreement comes to be with silent approval. In a new social situation, we quickly read the existing power structures off each other. We perceive these roles as being mutually agreed and, using various silent gestures, begin to monitor that everyone behaves according to expectations. In a similar way, you show your boss, coworkers, and customers how you allow yourself to be treated. Silent agreements can be difficult to change, but sometimes these invisible issues must be made visible, let the cat out of the bag, in order to renegotiate them.

For example, in my international company, we sometimes bring colleagues to Finland to speak at various events. For some reason, Finns have a silent agreement (or culture) that speakers are respected by keeping quiet; nobody makes questions or comments. The visitor must always be warned of this in advance. However, we are able to change this culture somewhat by beginning the event with casual conversation, by asking stupid questions, and by rewarding people who have questions - our aim is to create a silent agreement deviating from the tradition on how you can behave in this situation.

Power behind everything

Power means the ability to decide whether someone else gets what they want. For example, the customer has the power to decide whether your cooperation continues, but only if you wish to continue as well. The exercise of power can be either direct rewarding and punishment or indirect persuasion. On the face of it, power seems to determine who gets their way in a negotiation. However, the direct exercise of power in negotiations is challenging. If you **threaten** to exercise power, it is hard to step back from that threat without losing your credibility. The weaker form of a threat is a **warning**, the showing of power.

Do you wish to negotiate a better salary? For example, you can give your superior an ultimatum: "I received a job offer from a competitor with a monthly salary that is a thousand euros better than before. If I don't get the same here, I'll go with the competitor." The challenge with this threat is that you must be ready to go through with it, if necessary. Instead of threatening with a move to the competitor, you could show your power by giving a warning. For instance, you can bring up the fact that headhunters are actively contacting you.

In a company, power generally lies with three parties: the customers, the owners, and the employees. As the saying goes: "There is only one boss. The customer. And they can fire all employees of a company, starting with the Chairman of the Board, simply by taking their money elsewhere." However, ultimately, it is the owners who decide what a company does and only the employees have the ability to do it. The best way to increase your power is to help one of these parties gain more of it. Then they respectively give power to you when they have the authority. Salespeople get their power from the customers and specialists through their own expertise.

Even in an organization, the power is always exercised by a person. Even when decisions are publicly justified with the benefit of the company, a person who benefits from that benefit is always behind them. Therefore it is important to understand human needs. On radio channel Yle Puhe, Jari Sarasvuo (12 October 2015) presented a model of human needs that is more applicable to practical use than Maslow's hierarchy of needs. In the model, needs form a seesaw that is never balanced. When a person feels they are in control of things, life starts to feel too predictable, and they start to look for excitement, and vice versa. However, needs are individual. Some people look for more excitement than others and some prefer to feel in control. The first two levels of the model are of more priority than the third.

Need	Counterneed
Security feeling of control	**Excitement** change
Community joining	**Individuality** uniqueness
Success achievements	**Sharing** legacy

What is the superior's primary need in salary negotiations? We easily think of argumentation through the benefit of the company, but it may be that the boss does not care about salary costs - it is not their money after all. Maybe they want to keep you happy, so that they do not have to hire and train a new person to replace you, as this would mean a great deal of trouble for them personally. Here you may have a shared interest, for example, to increase the budget directed to the boss.

Room for negotiation

When sales have created an enticing cake, the negotiations on its sharing can begin. Negotiation usually leads to a deal. According to the rules of the free market economy, the creation of a deal is always a win-win situation for both parties. Neither party would make a deal unless the end result was better with the deal than without it. This does not mean, however, that the end result should be fair; if you are robbed, you may lose your money but keep your life, so both parties win.

COST ◀——ROOM FOR NEGOTIATION ——▶ EXPECTED VALUE

The price of the product or service you sell is always somewhere between the value received by the customer and the costs of your company. As you are (or at least the owner of your company is) likely to be looking for profit, you should be able to negotiate a deal with revenue exceeding your company's costs (at least in the long run). However, the customer is not willing to pay more than the value they are expecting to receive. The concrete costs are easy to calculate. There is more room for maneuver with value propositions. Value cannot usually be measured unambiguously. If the value is redeemed in the future, it involves insecurity, i.e. risk.

In its heyday, Nokia negotiated with subcontractors with the open book principle. Before Nokia agreed to negotiate, the subcontractor had to fill out a form revealing their cost and margin structure. That is, for example, the salaries for different roles or how much floor area was reserved for a certain number of employees in the office. Thus, the negotiation became a discussion about costs, which gave the subcontractor less room for negotiation.

BATNA ←——ROOM FOR NEGOTIATION——→ EXPECTED VALUE

The concept of BATNA (best alternative to a negotiated agreement) is often discussed in negotiation theory. It means the best alternative, if an agreement cannot be reached. So the room for negotiation in the line we have drawn is actually a lot smaller. We do not need to negotiate on a worse agreement than our best alternative. So evaluating your options is an important part of preparing for negotiations.

In Finland the strategy of many IT companies that survived the crash of Nokia's mobile phone operations was not to be a Nokia contractor, but to look for business elsewhere., Real choices give you room to breathe. If you give too much power to one party, it will suffocate you. Divide and conquer.

If you have a job offer from a competitor, it is easy to threaten your current employer with leaving. You are not willing to stay below the offered pay. However, threatening with a competing pay offer is ultimately a bad alternative, as you are maneuvering at the wrong end of the room for negotiation (in the minimum).

BATNA ←——ROOM FOR NEGOTIATION——→ BATNA

The opposite party also has their alternatives, for example, competitors to your company. Therefore, standing out from the competitors is vital. This limits the customer's alternatives. This is why companies construct solutions tailor-made to meet the customer's needs. Buyers on their part aim to deconstruct them to comparable sections that can be purchased separately from competitive market.

Simply standing out is naturally not enough, as you must also produce value. The best way to provide value and stand out at the same time is to create value through networks (demand side economics of scale), i.e. to own a standard. Say that a new Twitter of Facebook is trying to enter the market. It is hard for the newcomer to get users, as it has none. The first user cannot share their updates with anyone. When a second user joins, the service becomes much more valuable. And so forth. In this situation, the leading player is hard to copy, and the network provides growing value simultaneously. The winner takes it all.

What are your employer's options, if you leave? It may well be that your departure would incur bigger costs than raising your pay to exceed the offer from your competitor. From the employer's perspective, it is worth paying you a maximum of the alternative cost to the value you create.

Indirect methods

An engineer finds it easy to understand and analyze the direct exercise of power. However, the direct exercise of power will create a confrontation. Power is usually best kept hidden. Do not force the other party, if you can get them to want what you want.

The person drawing up the agenda for a meeting has hidden power, in regards to what is discussed, and the person keeping the minutes on how it is written down. Keeping the minutes is not a sought-after task, minutes are rarely checked carefully, and people generally do not remember exactly what was agreed. This means that the person keeping the minutes can shape the discussion in the direction they wish afterwards. I would recommend volunteering to keep the minutes, especially to those who feel they are trampled in a fast-paced discussion.

In his classic book, *Influence, Science and Practice*, Robert Cialdini presents the six principles of indirect influence. The basis is that the human mind does not have the time or the energy to logically analyze every situation. Our brain uses various shortcuts, stereotypes, and classifications that allow us to make automatic conclusions. These shortcuts generally lead to a useful end result, but they can also be consciously abused. For example, we automatically think that an expensive product is of better quality than a cheap one. Interrupting this automated deduction requires us to stop and identify it. But we do not always have the opportunity to do so. Our thoughts roll on at a hundred thousand thoughts per second.

1. Reciprocity

People have a strong need for reciprocity. Throughout history, individuals prone to reciprocity have survived and through evolution, we have developed an inherent need to return a favor. Reciprocity is a manner that enables cooperation. It creates trust, which frees us from constantly looking out for our own benefit. Still, it is important to recognize the conscious abuse of reciprocity. Turning down a gift usually causes more annoyance than not getting a gift in return.

Do favors and be helpful. It comes back to you with interest.

2. Consistency

Our culture values consistency. A person with unpredictable beliefs, statements, and actions is viewed as confused, unreliable, or even mentally ill. So we are under social pressure to be consistent. This pressure makes it hard to change an assumed role within a group. We have an automatic tendency to be consistent, even when this is not founded. It is easier to change opinion than behavior, and we often adjust our thinking afterwards to correspond with our actions. Studies show that people who are asked to mark a certain product as the best in a survey will most likely change their preferences accordingly.

Sell a whole in smaller pieces and let the customer justify the buying of the next piece to themselves, in order to guarantee consistency.

3. Social proof

Particularly in uncertain situations, we seek outside support for our decisions and trust the example of those we identify with. If we cannot remember how to eat a crawfish at a party, we look around and do as the others are doing. For the same reason, we tend to avoid empty restaurants. Reading the group is an easy way to save energy for the brain and usually results in a positive outcome. But, this automated process can also be easily abused.

The first followers are more important to a good leader than the leader's ability to inspire followers. See this video: www.youtube.com/watch?v=hO8MwBZl-Vc

4. Liking

Humans are social animals. We like and help especially those that belong to our group. We also tend to agree with people we like. Studies show that we are willing to change our opinion, if a person we hate agrees with us - not vice versa. Shared enemies unify the group. A similar phenomena is how we identify ourselves with the success of sports teams we support (WE won, but THEY lost).

Find the greatest common denominator and shared enemy to gain the customer's trust.

5. Authority

A group has a hierarchy and a leader. People are constantly observing signs about their status in the group and looking for a leader. In a study by Robert Cialdini, tall, handsome, suited men managed to lead three times as many people to cross a road at a red light than more scruffy-looking, studenty test persons. In the infamous experiments by Milgram at Yale University, most students were willing, under authority, to give nearly lethal electric shocks to subjects who appeared to be suffering and begged for mercy.

Communicate your position subtly with your clothing and appeal to authorities in your argumentation. Remember that the company you represent also provides you with authority.

6. Scarcity

We value scarcity. Tap water may cost approximately 1.5 euros per 1,000 liters, when the same amount of Norwegian VOSS water costs 15,000 euros, that is 10,000 times more. The unique is viewed to be more valuable than the freely available. The fear of loss is related to this phenomenon. People have a greater motivation to keep something old than to gain something new. This has been observed in anti-smoking campaigns. Appealing to the years lost due to smoking is much more efficient than appealing to the years gained by giving up smoking.

When selling, think whether there is a deadline for your offer or can the customer come back to the offer later without losing anything?

The existence of the distortions presented by Cialdini may be viewed as wrong and argue that decisions should be based on factual arguments. However, there is no use fighting human nature, this is how we are. But there is no point in exaggerating the chance for manipulation, as the methods of indirect influence are also part of normal interaction.

Negotiation style

We all have a negotiation style that suits us best. Some are not afraid of confrontation and tend to exercise more direct power, others are more conciliatory and know how to persuade the opposite party to use their power for their benefit. Different styles cannot be placed in order of preference; they all have their place. There is no use in acting against your personality. The most important thing is to be yourself and develop your negotiation skills, using the styles that work for you.

In *Bargaining for Advantage* Richard Shell divides the styles into the following categories:

Negotiation style	Description
The avoider	Aims to avoid situations where confrontation may appear.
The compromiser	Aims to find a fair solution quickly, while maintaining a good relationship with the opposite party.

The accommodator	Aims to quickly solve the opposite party's problem.
The competitor	Aims to win, regardless of the relationship with the opposite party. Own benefit comes first.
The problem solver	Aims to understand the problem and find the best possible solution for both parties.

In sales, the specialist often receives the role of the trusted advisor. This allows the person in charge of the commercial relationship to be more direct and the natural good cop/bad cop

scenario is created. This also makes it easier to trust the specialist. This does not mean, however, that the specialist should simply go along with the customer. Often the specialist is the correct person to challenge the customer's thinking.

Good cop/bad cop is an old interrogation technique, where one interrogator is threatening or inappropriate and the other is fair and understanding. This situation makes the subject prone to reveal information to the understanding and helpful interrogator.

The correct style for different situations is greatly dependent on the significance of the relationship. A magazine telemarketer can relentlessly push their special offers and not care about irritating potential customers. But usually, it is not advisable to risk a good customer relationship for a small sale. I personally feel that a good relationship, at least on a personal level, tends to be more valuable in the long run than an individual sale. Especially in a small country like Finland, bad behavior comes back to you sooner or later.

If the situation is hard for the employer, you may receive a pay rise by threatening to leave for a better salary elsewhere. However, you should think carefully how this threat will affect your work in the long run. In the worst case scenario, the employer gives you the raise, but once the difficult situation has passed, wants to get rid of you.

Richard Shell categorizes negotiation situations into four classes, based on the significance of the relationship between the parties. That is, how much the parties feel they will need each other in the future. And what is the size of the experienced conflict, how much do both parties want the same limited resource. Suitable alternatives from the above-mentioned negotiation styles can be selected for different situations based on this classification.

Balanced concerns: the relationship is important and conflict great, for example, a corporate fusion. Suitable approaches are:

1. Finding a creative solution
2. Compromise

Relationship: the relationship is important and the conflict small, for example, a romantic relationship. Suitable approaches are:

1. Finding a creative solution
2. Compromise
3. Accommodation

Transaction: relationship is not important and the conflict great, for example, the sale of a car. Suitable approaches are:

1. Finding a creative solution
2. Competition
3. Compromise

Tacit coordination: relationship is not important and the conflict is small, for example, driving order at a crossroads. Suitable approaches are:

1. Avoiding
2. Accommodation
3. Compromise

Negotiation process

The negotiation process ties everything discussed above into a useful tool. In his book, Richard Shell presents a negotiation process in four stages. A simplified example is two cars meeting at a crossroads: slowing down and observing the situation (1. preparing), signaling who goes first (2. exchanging information), wave with the hand, a nod (3. opening and making concessions), and finally driving as agreed (4. commitment).

1. Preparing your strategy

As with many other activities, in a negotiation, the result is first and foremost dependent on preparation. You can start your preparation by observing the negotiation situation, based on the described classification. How important do you view the relationship with the other party to be in the future and how great is the conflict of interests? You can also view the situation from the opposite party's perspective. How do they view the importance of the relationship and the conflict? Could the opposite party's view be adapted through persuasion? Based on this delibera-tion, you can build your plan for the negotiations.

> **Negotiation style.** What is the negotiation style that works for the situation and for you? Should someone else negotiate, if the situation de-mands a style that is not among your strengths?

> **Goals and expectations.** What is your goal? And what are your expectations? Could prepa-ration bring your expectations, that is what you believe you should receive, closer to the goals?

> **Norms and standards**. Are there standards or practices effecting the negotiation that you can appeal to or against which you should be pre-pared to argue? For example, the brokerage commission in real estate has been established at a certain percentage of the real estate price, even though it is not necessarily justifiable.

Relationship. How significant is the relationship to you? And to the other party? Can you use persuasion methods to affect the significance felt by the other party?

Needs of the opposite party. Who is the decision-maker on the other side? Do you have shared goals? How could you reaching your goals help the opposite party? What could prevent you from reaching a deal? Why would the opposite party say no? Look for ways to solve the opposite party's problems, while promoting your own case.

Power and leverage. What alternatives do you and the opposite party have? Who controls the current situation and who is looking for a change? On whose side is time? What kind of rewarding and punishing power do you have on the opposite party?

A goal gives the direction to the negotiations, but expectations, what you believe you should get, guide your behavior. Expectations are formed based on previous experiences, perceptions, information, and our personality. In preparing for negotiations, you should focus especially on gathering information that supports the belief that the goal is justifiable and realistic. Knowing the minimum of your room for negotiation gives you support, but be careful that it does not turn into an attractive reference point. Define your goals specifically and in writing. They are worth discussing with other people. The stronger you believe in and commit to your goals, the stronger you will hold on to them in a negotiation situation.

Imagine two drivers heading towards each other on a single-track road. One removes the steering wheel and throws it out the window. Which driver is more likely to give way? This is a dirty tactic that can be used in negotiations, for example, by publicly committing to a goal. A trade union negotiator could tell the press they would resign, if they cannot achieve a pay rise of at least 5%.

2. Exchanging information

At this stage, the plan is carefully taken into action, the building of a relationship begins, assumptions are tested, information is gathered, and goals and authority communicated.

3. Opening and making concessions

Here we have identified the other party's goals, problems and presumptions and start to look for a solution. This stage involves three questions:

1. Is it wise to open with an offer? The general rule is never to make an offer first. Let the other party open. They may make a better offer than you have expected, and if not, you can always reply with a counter-offer. However, by opening you may be able to set a reference point that guides subsequent negotiations. The best way to ensure that you do not make a mistake with opening is only to negotiate with parties that feel that they have a significant relationship to you.

2. Is it better to make an optimistic or a reasonable offer? If the relationship is significant, the answer is clear: make a reasonable offer. Studies show that in a competitive situation, it is best to make the highest (or lowest, i.e. best for you) offer you can justify. A high offer acts as a beneficial comparison and contrast for negotiation and allows for mutual concessions.

3. What kind of concession works best? Mutual concession always feels better than a direct agreement on a reasonable outcome. After a good negotiation, you can be sure of a good deal. You know how it feels when your offer goes through directly? Could you have received more? A tried and tested negotiation strategy is as follows: make an optimistic offer, hold on to it for a while, show you are willing to negotiate, make concessions step by step, make the steps smaller as you begin to reach your expectation level.

4. Closing and gaining commitment

The negotiation process ends at a situation where the purpose is to establish a final decision and commitment to the end result. This stage often involves different tactics, such as ultimatums and withdrawals that create pressure to make the decision. Amidst the pressure, you should also ensure that the other party is committed to what is agreed. Here, leverage lies with the party that feels they will lose less, if the deal does not go through, has time on their side, and is less committed to the negotiation process.

A skilled buyer takes advantage of the fact that the seller is more committed to the sales process than the buyer. The seller may have devoted so much time to the sales project that they must make a deal or they will miss their sales targets. Knowing this makes it easy for the buyer to demand discounts. So, it is important that the seller and buyer commit to cooperation at the same pace. For example, this may mean that the customer pays something for proof of concept, instead of getting it for free.

Deepening the cooperation

Cooperation begins with a deal. However, the deal is simply a starting point. After reaching an agreement, you must ensure that people commit to it. This involves various rituals, declarations, and contractual responsibilities, but it is also important to organize procedures for monitoring the implementation and managing the cooperation.

The first sale is only a beginning of cooperation. It acts as an internal reference, when you begin to construct the customer relationship. Next, you can chart decision-makers, get to know the customer strategy and organization, and look for suitable targets for your next deal. Then you can create a sales project case that helps you deepen the customer relationship. At the latest, when you have several deliveries, it is wise to build a common steering group with the customer. This is how your relationship with the customer and especially their top management becomes deeper. Little by little, you are included in strategic projects and can spar their plans for the future. In the end, you are your customer's strategic partner.

Interview: Taina Närhi

Taina Närhi has had a long career in the graphic industry and she is also a sales and marketing professional. During her career, she has managed projects in very technical environments. Taina has studied in Scotland as a Scotwork negotiation coach and has taught negotiation skills for over 10 years with her company Face Value Oy.

Why is negotiating so important?

Negotiating is an important skill for everyone, both in professional and personal situations. Negotiation is a funny concept in that many people say they do not need negotiation skills in their work. However, everyone negotiates. We face internal negotiations, external negotiations, customer negotiations and other situations daily, where promoting our goals is necessary or at least desirable.

Negotiation skills are needed in acquisitions, sales, HR, and management tasks, among others. Negotiation is not just argumentation about the matter at hand, but above all discretion, promoting the cause, charting the obstacles and priorities of the other party with correct questions, and constructing a motivating suggestion for the other party, in order to reach a result.

Negotiating is barter trade, where you exchange something not so important to you for something that is important to the other party. So I can let go of something in order to get the opposite party moving and committing to a shared goal. Building a good negotiation culture in a company saves time, produces better results, and creates more confident negotiators. Therefore, management and HR should include the development of negotiation skills as a primary development target.

The weakness of engineers?

Technical specialists are particularly excited about their own product, technology, and equipment, and that is the main message to the customer. It is their strength in what they do. Salespeople are also excited about finalizing a sale. But sometimes this excitement can surpass the customer benefit in a way that does not entice the customer to commit to the project. The customer is uncertain about how the technical solution will develop their efficiency or business.

People who make decisions about money have their own language. Savings and benefits speak to them. And the customer will want to talk about these issues. What is the bottleneck of production? What kind of challenges are there in the operating environment? These are the questions the customer likes to answer. Then you can adapt your offering to the customer need.

Sufficient discussion (argumentation) opens up a great number of opportunities and elements for negotiation.

It can also be considered a weakness, if you are too willing to touch issues that are important to you, such as the price. Good preparation allows you to find other methods that motivate the customer to reach the end result. Technical people tend to think creatively, and negotiation is a creative art.

Your tips for engineers?

Preparation. Study your negotiation partner. And above all, define your goals, priorities, bargaining points, and the information you need from the other party to reach your targets in advance. Yet another tip for meeting with the opposite party: two ears and one mouth.

I would recommend studying the stages involved in negotiations, either through literature or by taking a course that opens up all stages of a negotiation process. A negotiation is first and foremost a process, the course of which is important to identify. The structure of negotiations is universal, though the building of trust may differ from culture to culture. You become a good negotiator by practicing, not by repeating the same formula.

In conclusion

IMAGE: THE STRUCTURE OF THE BOOK

Why should we sell?

We have now covered the entire sales process from opening the discussion to building trust and further through emotions and logic into negotiations. But, why exactly do we need these skills? Is learning to sell simply a good choice for your own employment and career or could it serve some greater purpose?

This cannot go on

We are in an unsustainable situation in Finland and around the world:

1. Economically

Intensifying international competition and automation will decrease the number of jobs in the Western world, which chips away at the financial base of our well-being. An aging population places further pressure on our public services and their funding.

2. Socially

Digitalization and robotization strongly polarize economic well-being. Inequality has increased in the Western countries. This threatens to diminish the social cohesion needed for sustainable well-being.

3. Ecologically

Climate change and dwindling natural resources will force us to change our operations. The limits of Earth's capacity are showing. We cannot continue to live at the expense of future generations and the poorest people of the world.

All is better than before

The UN evaluates that poverty has been reduced more in the past 50 years than in the prior 500 years, and that child mortality has more than halved since 1990. More children also have the chance to go to school. According to the UN, less than one in ten children receives no basic education.

In the 1980s of my childhood, Finland was more closely tied to the Soviet Union than Europe. We had no mobile phones or internet connections. At the end of the 19th century, people actually starved in Finland and a civil war took place less than a hundred years ago.

Development keeps on developing

There is much talk of the fourth industrial revolution, which will reorganize not only the business world, but the society as a whole.

According to KPMG's Global CEO Outlook study published in October 2016, 72% of CEOs think that the coming three years are more crucial and decisive for business than the past 50 years.

In the report *Technology as an enabler of sustainable well-being in the modern society* published by Sitra, Risto Linturi lists the following 10 technologies as the most central drivers of change in society.

1. Virtual reality

The physical world becomes available through virtual reality. Telepresence allows for work to be organized regardless of physical location. Services can be offered to Finland from India, for example.

2. Artificial intelligence

A large share of the work of doctors or lawyers, for example, can be automated by using artificial intelligence. Artificial intelligence can make previously expensive professional services inexpensive and accessible to everyone.

3. Sensors

Inexpensive sensors can soon be used to study air quality, food content, biometrics, or even DNA structure. Sensors allow for the automated and predictive diagnostics of illnesses.

4. Robotized transport

Driverless cars turn transport into a service. Robotized transport and logistics can transform trade and the urban environment.

5. Robotized production and 3D printing

Automated production makes small production batches profitable and increases the number of different alternatives. Production moves closer to the consumers and the traditional value chain of mass production is turned upside down. Peer production and social commons, for example, freely printable 3D models, may become an important part of production.

6. Nanomaterials

New materials may replace old ones, such as plastic and metal. For example, graphene's tensile strength makes it 300 times stronger than steel. At the same time, it is an extremely light and flexible material with high electrical conductivity. Furthermore, graphene can at best be produced from carbon dioxide in the atmosphere, thus decreasing climate change.

7. Biotechnology and pharmacology

Sensors and artificial intelligence may allow us to achieve self-sufficiency by growing our own food at home. Pharmacological development will increase our life expectancy to over 100 years.

8. Energy technology

Solar power is quickly becoming less expensive. Fraunhofer Institutes estimate that solar power will reach the current electricity price level in 80% of countries by 2017. Several researches estimate that by 2050 the cost of solar electricity will drop to 2-4 cents per kWh, which is the same level as the current transmission cost of electricity in Finland.

9. Digital platforms

New digital platforms enable new types of cooperation and replace traditional operators. Uber, Airbnb, eBay, Paypal, Bitcoin, Kickstarter, Shapeways, Linux and Wikipedia are but a few examples of what a sharing economy, peer production, crowdfunding, etc. can mean in the future.

10. Globalization of ICT

Many of the new platforms and services will integrate into global companies whose operation can be difficult to govern by the local legislation of individual countries. This demands wider cooperation.

Selling is our obligation

We have achieved incredible well-being by specializing and working together.

When we do not have to worry about growing our food or about our safety, we can dedicate our efforts to the development of technology, for example.

The market economy has proven itself to be a functioning and flexible way to define worthwhile specialization areas and cooperation partners.

The market economy and free competition promote development and protect us from capitalist monopolies. Selling is the motor of the market economy.

Technology is developing and changing the world at an increasing speed. We cannot stop or turn around. The more we embrace the change and utilize it, the better we will cope.

Technology can also solve our unsustainable challenges regarding the economy, inequality, and the environment. The development of technology is our ultimate hope.

Selling implements this development by helping societies understand new, more sustainable ways of working and by encouraging us to beat the insecurity created by change.

Selling technology is our moral obligation.

Happy Selling!

Janne V. Korhonen
In Helsinki, 31. October 2016

References and recommended reading

22 Immutable Laws of Marketing, Al Ries & Jack Trout

Aristoteles Hollywoodissa, Ari Hiltunen

Bargaining for Advantage: Negotiation Strategies for Reasonable People, Richard Shell

Beyond Reason: Using Emotions as You Negotiate, Roger Fisher & Daniel Shapiro

Getting to Yes with Yourself: And Other Worthy Opponents, William Ury

Getting to Yes: Negotiating an Agreement Without Giving In, Roger Fisher & William Ury

Gurumarkkinointi, Jari Parantainen

Growth Hacker Marketing, Ryan Holiday

Influence: The Psychology of Persuasion, Robert Cialdini

Innovation and Entrepreneurship, Peter Drucker

Linchpin, Seth Godin

Markkinoinnin automaatio 2.0., Digitys

Made to Stick: Why Some Ideas Survive and Others Die, Chip Heath & Dan Heath

Mastering Technical Sales, John Care & Aron Bohlin

Matketing Spirit, Petri Parvinen

Mielipidejohtaja - Voittajan resepti toimialasi valloitukseen, Jarkko Kurvinen & Lauri Sipilä

Myyntipsykologia, Petri Parvinen

Miten minusta tuli huippuluokan myyjä, Frank Bettger

Neuvotteluvalta, Juhana Torkki & Sami Miettinen

Ostovallankumous, Mika Rubanovitsch & Jukka Aminoff

Outboundista Inboundiin, Advance B2B

Ostajapersoonat, Advance B2B

Pitch Anything, Oren Klaff

Puhevalta, Juhana Torkki

Puhevalta käyttöön, Juhana Torkki

Presentation Zen: Simple Ideas on Presentation Design and Delivery, Garr Reynolds

Sissimarkkinointi, Jari Parantainen

Social Selling Opas, Advance B2B

Smart Selling on The Phone and Online,: Inside Sales That Gets Results, Josiane Chriqui Feigon & Jill Konrath

Story: Style, Structure, Substance, and the Principles of Screenwriting, Robert McKee

Tarinan valta, Juhana Torkki

Thinking, Fast and Slow, Daniel Kahneman

Thank You for Arguing, Jay Heinrichs

The Art of Social Media, Guy Kawasaki & Peg Fitzpatrick

The Challenger Sale, How to Take Control of Customer Conversation, Matthew Dixon & Brent Adamson

The Challenger Customer: Selling to the Hidden Influencer Who Can Multiply Your Results, Brent Adamson & Matthew Dixon

The Naked Presenter: Delivering Powerful Presentations With or Without Slides, Garr Reynolds

The Trusted Advisor Sales Engineer, John Care

To Sell is Human: The Surprising Truth About Persuading, Convincing, and Influencing Others, Daniel Pink

Traction: How Any Startup Can Achieve Explosive Customer Growth, Gabriel Weinberg

Winning Arguments From Aristotle to Obama - Everything You Need to Know About the Art of Persuasion, Jay Heinrichs

Made in the USA
Coppell, TX
04 October 2020